GIRAFFES

by Michèle Dufresne

Pioneer Valley Educational Press, Inc.

Here is a **giraffe**.

Giraffes are tall.
Look at the tall giraffes!

A giraffe's **legs**
can be six feet long.

A giraffe's **neck**
can be six feet long.

The giraffe is hungry.
The giraffe is **eating** leaves
on a tall tree.

Look at the giraffe's **spots**.

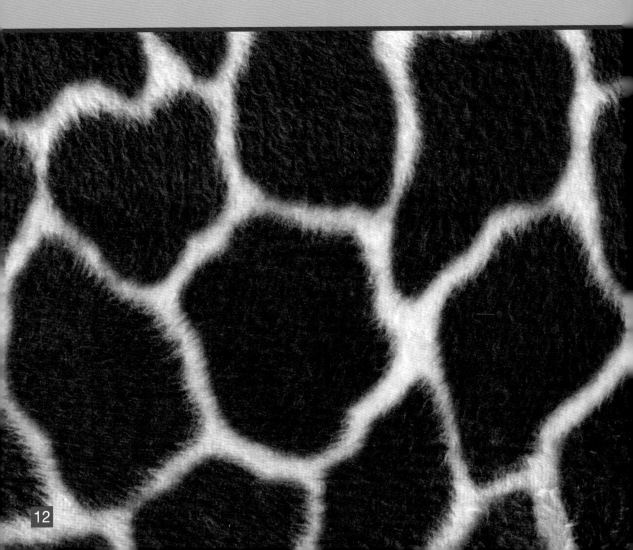

Look at the giraffe's **horns**.

Here is a baby giraffe.
The baby giraffe is called
a **calf**.

GIRAFFES

neck

eating

calf

legs

horns

spots

giraffe